## OF THIS WORLD
### A POET'S LIFE IN POETRY

# OF THIS WORLD
## A POET'S LIFE IN POETRY
by RICHARD LEWIS
Photographs by HELEN BUTTFIELD

THE DIAL PRESS, INC. New York

895.6

The editor would like to thank the following for their permission to reprint poems and passages found in this book: The Hokuseido Press, Tokyo, for *A History of Haiku* translated by R. H. Blyth. University of California Press for *Year of My Life* by Issa translated by Nobuyuku Yuasa, 1960. Hallmark Cards, Incorporated and The Hokuseido Press for *Haiku* translated by R. H. Blyth. © Hallmark Cards, Incorporated. Reprinted by permission.

The editor would also like to thank the following authors and their publishers for information regarding the life of Issa: Lewis Mackenzie, editor and author of *The Autumn Wind,* published by John Murray, Ltd., London. Max Beckerton, editor and author of *Issa's Life and Poetry,* published in *Transactions, Asiatic Society of Japan.*

Lastly, the editor would like to acknowledge the translations of bibliographic material by Miss Umeyo Hirano and translations of biographic material by Miss Haruna Kimura.

Text copyright © 1968 by Richard Lewis
Photographs copyright © 1968 by Helen Buttfield Hartman
All rights reserved. No part of this book may be reproduced in any form or by any means without the prior written permission of the Publisher, excepting brief quotes used in connection with reviews written specifically for inclusion in a magazine or newspaper.
Library of Congress Catalog Card Number: 68-28739
Printed in the United States of America

*First Printing*

TO AMANDA
whose first breath has brought
us closer to first things...

Richard and Nancy Lewis

# INTRODUCTION

The lives of most men, when held up to public view, reflect only a series of events. Added together, the events make up a lifetime. But within and around these events there are the feelings, experiences, and visions which few men ever show to each other, but which are actually the very core of their lives. Every so often there is a man who is not content to allow his life to pass into the silence of mere events. He is compelled, through some means, to express what is within him. He must, rather than remain alone with his thoughts and feelings, share this inner world with others. His response to life, even after he has died, must become part of the lives of those who still live.

One such man was Issa, a poet who lived in Japan in the eighteenth century. This book tells the story of the lifetime which was his world. It is a story told in two ways. At the beginning of each of the four sections of the book, I have given the basic facts of Issa's life—facts which relate, to the best of our knowledge, the external events which shaped his life as a person and a poet. These biographical sections are purposely short and are meant to be no more than an introduction to the various poems by Issa. These I have arranged to follow the course of his inner life. This poetic arrangement does not parallel the events of Issa's life from year to year. It is a means of exploring his expression of some of the moments of his life which found their way into his poetry. The poems were not chosen and put into the various sequences of the book because of their date of composition but rather for their quality and the way they convey a particular mood, feeling, time, or event compatible with a particular period of Issa's life. Essentially these poems should be thought of as images strung together to reveal the inner world of a man whose whole life was a struggle to react to the mystery of existence through the expression of a poem.

The poetical aspect of Issa's story is deeply compelling because of the very nature of the poetry he wrote, a form known as haiku. This form, developed over many centuries in Japan, is a precise seventeen-syllable poem. Like many of the delicate Japanese ink drawings, haiku uses clear outlines of thought in order to convey a multitude of images, moods, and sensations. Every word is carefully balanced by every other word and no word, thought, or image is ever used to excess. In one respect a haiku poem is like a tree in winter without leaves, suggesting through its shape, nakedness, and the imagination of the reader what it will look like, full-bloom, in the summer. What is not said in a haiku poem is as important as what is said—or as one poet put it: "It is a hand beckoning, a door half-opened, a mirror wiped clean."

Issa inherited the haiku form after it had been refined by great poets like Basho and Buson. He carried on the tradition of haiku writing with a style uniquely his own. To many people he is the most human of all the haiku poets. As one contemporary said of him: "He intentionally keeps one foot planted in the dust of the world, and the range of his human sympathies is far greater than can adequately be described."

Yet what made Issa the man that he was can never really be described. His life, by ordinary standards, was tragic. Yet his poetry sings with a beauty few poets at any time have ever surpassed. Even in poems which portray moments of his own despair, he never lost his hold upon the wonder and richness of life around him. No creature is too small for his attention, no movement of the wind or passing shadow escapes him, no subtlety of texture or mood eludes him—everything becomes deeply part of his own entirety: himself.

His poetry lives on today because of his gift of allowing us to participate along with him in his own discovery of being alive. And through that discovery we, like Issa, realize that "happiness and sorrow are roped into one." We travel in the presence of a man whose greatest journey was his own life and who was able to see reflections of that life in all things at all times. We are able, through the eyes, feelings, and thoughts of a great man and poet, to understand something of what it means to be fully human and very much a part of this world.

R.L.
May 1968

# PART 1

The man we shall know as Issa was born and named Yataro on May 5, 1763, in the small mountain village of Kashiwabara in northern Japan. Although May 5 is traditionally the Day of the Iris Festival, when carp banners are flown over every household blessed with sons, no banners flew over the household of Yataro. His family was too busy reaping rice from its fields, and, as Yataro later tells us, around his cradle planting songs were sung instead of lullabies. Yataro's father, Yagobei, was a hard-working farmer, and for the first few years of Yataro's life there was little hardship. But this was not to last long, and the first of many tragedies of Yataro's life occurred when he was three years old. His mother, Kuni, suddenly died, and his grandmother, Kanajo, took over the role of mother. She did the best she could but from Yataro's writing later on we gather that she was withdrawn, and that his father, alone without a wife, did not talk very much to the rest of the family. Yataro goes on to tell us that he himself became sullen and found it difficult to play with the children of the village, preferring to play by himself in the woods and fields near his home.

When Yataro was six he was sent to a village school run by Rokuzaemon Nakamura, who was also master of the village inn, a wine merchant, and a poet. In time Yataro gained a reputation in the village as a good student and was encouraged to develop his gifts in every way. Two years later his father married a woman named Satsu, who resented the time Yataro spent on his studies instead of working hard on the land. She soon convinced his father to take Yataro out of school. The differences between Yataro and his stepmother grew worse every day, to the point where she would not even allow him light to read by at night. When Satsu gave birth to her son Senroku, Yataro was asked to look after the infant, only to be blamed every time the child cried. Yataro, in one of his diaries, said of this time: "I was whipped a hundred times a day— a thousand times a month" and "never slept without shedding tears."

His father, in desperation over the endless quarrels in his family, decided to send Yataro to Edo (now Tokyo). On a spring morning in 1776, when Yataro was thirteen years old, he and his father secretly left the house and walked to a neighboring town, where Yataro joined some travelers on their way to Edo. His father left him with these words: "Eat nothing harmful, don't let people think any ill of you, and let me see your healthy face again." Yataro sat in silence for some time, nodded, and then bowed his farewell.

Clear, cold water
Straight
From the mountain
Into my tub.

The smoke
Is now making
The first sky of the year.

Now I am going out;
Be good and play together,
Crickets.

Among the leaves of grass,
The frogs
    Are playing hide-and-seek.




            Look, snail,
        Look, O look,
            At your own shadow!

Mossy clear water!
Come on now, pigeons!
　　Come on now, sparrows!

　　　　　　　　　　　Let's ride
　　　　　　　　On the duck-weed flowers
　　　　　　　　　　To the clouds over there.

Little sparrow,
Mind, mind, out of the way,
Mr. Horse is coming.

"It's silly for the day to be so long!"
Says the crow
Opening its mouth.

The first firefly!
It was off, away—
The wind left in my hand.

    Today also, today also,
Living in the haze—
    A small house.


    By the light of the next room,
I sit before my small food-table;
    Ah, the cold.

A world of short-lived dew,
And in that dewdrop—
  What violent quarrels!

A scarecrow
Shields
A child
From the autumn wind.

How happy, how affectionate they are!
If I am reborn, may I be
  A butterfly in the fields.




  Come and play with me,
Fatherless, motherless
    Sparrow.

An exhausted sparrow
In the midst
   Of a crowd of children.

30

An autumn evening;
It is no light thing,
To be born a man.

# PART 2

When Yataro arrived in Edo he found a bustling, extravagant city where even the dialect, with its clipped slang, confused him. It seemed no place for someone like Yataro, with his slow country speech and ways. It is not clear how he survived, but he wrote later that for many days he was cold, hungry, and without a place to sleep. He may possibly have earned some money by working as a stable boy, doing clerical work, or being an apprentice in one of the big mansions that could be found throughout Edo at the time.

It was not until 1787 that we have some documentary evidence of what Yataro was doing. In that year he signed his name to a handwritten exercise book which he completed as part of his training as a poet in the school of haiku taught by Nirokuan. After Nirokuan died, Yataro, at the age of twenty-seven, succeeded him as head of the school. Yataro resigned from the post after less than a year.

Haunted by a dream that his father had fallen under bad influences, Yataro walked home in 1791, for the first time since his arrival in Edo. To his relief his father was in good health, and subsequently Yataro planned a journey throughout Japan. Taking such a journey was a part of poetic tradition which many haiku poets undertook in order to become more proficient at writing through the solitude of wandering.

It was at this time that Yataro took on the name of Issa, his whole name being Haikaiji Nyudo Issa-bo, which means Brother Issa, Lay Priest of the Temple of Poetry. Having shaved his head, wearing a priestly costume, and carrying a pilgrim's staff, he began to walk the length and breadth of Japan, meeting other poets, and reading and writing haiku.

Not until 1798 did Issa go back to Edo, where, in old and dusty clothes, he attended haiku meetings, earned a little money from teaching, and accepted the pleasures of knowing that his reputation as a poet was increasing. In 1801 he left Edo again for his native village, arriving just in time to nurse his father through the last days of his life.

Wild goose, O wild goose,
Your first journey—
　　How old were you?

Making his way through the crowd,
In his hand
A poppy.

"Country bumpkin"
People call me—
　　How cold it is!

In this fleeting world
Even the little bird
    Makes himself a nest.

Eating a meal
In loneliness,
　　　The autumn wind blowing.

　　　　　The full moon;
My ramshackle hut
　　Is as you see it.

Just being here,
I am here,
And the snow falls.

The wren
Earns his living
Noiselessly.

Round my hut
Even grasses
　　　Suffer from summer thinness.


　　　　　　　　　Insects are crying;
　　　　　　　A hole in the wall
　　　　　　　　　Not seen yesterday.


　　　　　A beautiful kite
　　　Rose from
　　　　　The beggar's hovel.

Where are you going,
Little pilgrim?
To where the autumn winds blow.

An autumn evening;
A man on a journey
　　　Sewing his clothes.




　　　　　　　　I borrowed the wayside shrine
　　　　　　From the fleas and mosquitoes
　　　　　　　　And went to sleep.

A thousand
Plovers
Rise
As one.

Ill on a journey;
My dreams wander
　　Over a withered moor.

Click, clack,
The man coming walking in the haze—
Who is he?

On a cool evening
Of summer
I see the same old tree
Standing by the gate.

Whose cottage
Can it be
Beyond this
Moss-grown spring?

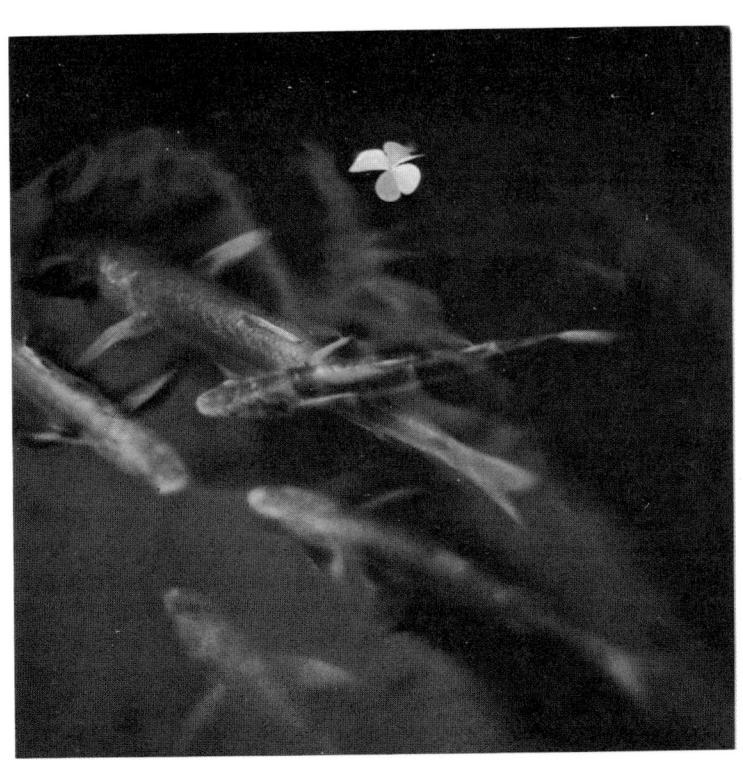

Tonight, in the sky,
Even the stars
Seem to whisper
To one another.

# PART 3

Very soon after Issa returned to his village, his father contracted typhoid fever. While Issa did his best to relieve his father's pain, very little could be done to prevent his death, which occurred on May 20. Issa wrote of that day: "I felt I lost the only light in the complete darkness. Innocent spring flowers scattered by the cruel wind. A beautiful moon was covered by dark clouds."

    Before his father died he had made Issa vow that he would marry and settle down in their village. In return his father promised Issa a part of the family property. Disputes with his stepmother and stepbrother arose again—this time over the dividing of the land. Issa felt that there was nothing left for him to do amid such arguments but to return to Edo. Although his reputation as a poet had increased there, he still lived in great poverty. While in Edo he tried to settle his family problems. Finally, after seven years had passed, his stepbrother gave him a written document stating that the family property would be divided as requested by his father. Leaving Edo in 1812, Issa went back to the village, where the matter was settled once and for all. Not only was the land divided, a wall was put up in the middle of the house.

    In 1814, at the age of fifty-one, Issa married a woman named Kiku, who was twenty-seven and the daughter of a farmer from a neighboring village. Their first son, Konzo, was born two years later, but died within a month. Another son was born the following year and also died within a month. Their hopes for another child were realized in 1818 when a daughter, Sato, was born. She began to grow into a healthy and beautiful child. In one of his journals Issa said of her: "She seems just like a butterfly, poised lightly on a sprig of young spring grass, resting her wings." Again, in the same journal, he gives another picture of her:

"…the moonlight touched her gate, adding a breath of coolness to the evening air. A group of children dancing outside suddenly lifted their voices and cried aloud. My little girl at once threw down the little bowl she had been playing with and crawled out to the porch, where she, too, cried out and stretched forth her hands to the moon."
Suddenly, when she was a year old, she was stricken with smallpox. Of this Issa writes:
"Being, as I am, her father, I can scarcely bear to watch her withering away —a little more each day—like some pure, untainted blossom that is ravished by the sudden onslaught of mud and rain."
Death was inevitable. Issa continues:
"She grew weaker and weaker, and finally on the twenty-first of June, as the morning glories were closing their flowers, she closed her eyes forever. Her mother embraced the cold body and cried bitterly. For myself —I knew well it was no use to cry, that water once flown past the bridge does not return, and blossoms that are scattered are gone beyond recall. Yet try as I would, I could not, simply could not cut the binding cord of human love."

Were my father here,
At dawn we would gaze
Over the green fields.

Visiting the graves;
The old dog
    Leads the way.

 

Heat waves;
It haunts my eyes—
    His laughing face.

My old home;
Getting near, or touching it,
Flowers of the thorny
briar.

Little garden at the gate,
Just the thing for you—
   This evening shower!

The cool breeze
Finds a home
　　Even in a single blade of grass.

In the shade of the thicket,
A woman by herself,
　　Singing the planting song.

A day of spring;
Twilight lingers
　　　Wherever there is water.

The wind gives us
All the dry leaves
We need
For our little household.



In our house
The mice are friendly
With the fireflies.

The feeble plant,
At last,
   Has a wobbly flower.

Ah! to be
A child—
On New Year's Day!

Crawl, laugh,
Do as you wish—
For you are one year old
This morning.

The child sobs,
"Give it to me!"
The bright full moon.

She has put the child to sleep,
And now washes the clothes;
The summer moon.

In the dream
My daughter
Lifts a melon
Up to her soft cheek.

Spring rain—
A few ducklings
Left over from the winter
Cry on the lake.

                                        The autumn breeze;
                          Scarlet flowers blooming
                                            The dead girl wished to pluck.

The world of dew
Is the world of dew,
And yet...
And yet...

# PART 4

In the last years of Issa's life one misfortune followed another. Very soon after Sato died, another son was born but lived for only a few months. In the same year Issa himself was attacked by the paralysis which was to plague him throughout the rest of his life. After the birth of another son, his wife, Kiku, fell ill and died in the spring of 1823. This fourth son also died in infancy—supposedly because of the carelessness of the woman Issa employed to care for the child.

In 1824, Issa married again, but this union lasted only a few weeks. His paralysis reappeared, and it became increasingly difficult for him to speak.

Then, at the age of sixty-three, he married once more. In the summer of 1827, a fire destroyed Issa's house, and he and his wife, Yao, had to live in the storehouse of their farm, which had neither a window nor a chimney.

One day, after a walk in the snow, paralysis overtook Issa again, and he died at the age of sixty-five. He was buried among the family graves on top of the hill of his native village. His gravestone bears this inscription:

> Is this it, then,
> My last resting place—
> Five feet of snow!

In the following spring a child was born to Issa's widow. This was the only one of his children to reach maturity.

If only she were here,
My complaining partner—
Today's moon.

The coolness
Of the sound of water at night,
Falling back into the well.

The autumn wind;
The shadow of the mountain
　　Trembles.

The beggar on the bridge
also
Calls to the fireflies:
He has a child.

A butterfly came,
And flew off
   With a butterfly in the garden.

The short night;
A scarlet flower has bloomed
At the tip of the vine.

The moorhens are chirping,
And to their beat
    The clouds are hurrying, hurrying!




                    How much
            Are you enjoying yourself,
                    Tiger moth?

As we grow old,
Even the length of the day
Is a cause of tears.

Getting colder,
The song of the earthworm also
Dwindles every evening.

After a flock of flies
Has escaped its blows,
This wrinkled hand.

In my old age,
Even before the scarecrow
I feel ashamed of myself!

The autumn wind;
There are thoughts
   In the mind of Issa.

As one of us,
The cat is seated here;
The parting year.

Come out, fireflies!
I'm going to lock up—
Do come out!

Be a good boy
And look after the house well,
Cricket!

Dewdrops on the grass,
 Are you falling on me—
Me, still alive?

With feeble steps
The old man
Totters by —
To look at flowers.


The woodpecker,
Still pecking at the same place.
The day draws to its close.

In the wintry grove,
Echoes
Of long, long ago.

| DATE DUE | | |
|---|---|---|
| ~~SEP 25 72~~ JAN 30 1974 *Walgren* 2e | | |

895.6

Lewis
OF THIS WORLD

DISCARDED

Chief Joseph School